Table of Contents

Table of Contents

1 Spectral Gardening Basics

The very essence of spectral gardening lies in understanding the unique properties of quantum soil. Unlike the earthly soil we are familiar with, quantum soil possesses a heightened sensitivity to spectral energies, acting as a conduit for the ethereal whispers of the cemetery. Preparing this unique medium requires a delicate touch and an understanding of its subtle energetic properties. Begin by gathering soil from the cemetery grounds, ensuring it is rich in the essence of the departed. This soil, infused with the memories and energies of past lives, forms the foundation of your spectral garden. Mix this earthen base with finely ground quartz crystals, chosen for their ability to amplify and channel spectral energies. The crystals act as miniature antennas, drawing in the ambient energies of the cemetery and focusing them within the soil. Finally, incorporate crushed phosphorescent minerals. These minerals, with their inherent capacity to absorb and re-emit light, will imbue the soil with a gentle, otherworldly glow, providing a constant source of spectral energy for your nascent flora.

Cemetery energetics play a vital role in the success of your spectral garden. These locations, steeped in the history of lives lived and lost, possess a unique energetic signature, a confluence of earthly and spectral energies. To effectively harness these energies, you must first learn to attune yourself to the subtle vibrations of the cemetery. Spend time within its confines, meditating amongst the tombstones, allowing yourself to become receptive to the whispers of the departed. Observe the natural flow of energy within the cemetery. Notice areas where the energy seems to pool or flow more freely. These are the power points, the ideal locations for your spectral garden. By understanding the ebb and flow of these energies, you can position your garden to maximize its absorption of spectral power, fostering the growth of truly luminescent flora. The cemetery's energy is not static; it fluctuates with the cycles of the moon, the changing seasons, and even the time of day. Learning to recognize and work with these fluctuations is key to mastering spectral gardening.

Spectral seed selection is perhaps the most crucial aspect of spectral gardening. Not just any seed will thrive in this unique environment. You must seek out seeds that possess an inherent affinity for the spectral realm, seeds that resonate with the energies of the cemetery. Look for seeds gathered from plants that thrive in liminal spaces – those in-between places where the veil between worlds is thin. Plants that grow in graveyards, near ancient ruins, or along the edges of forgotten pathways often hold the potential for spectral luminescence. These seeds, imbued with the subtle energies of these liminal spaces, are more likely to flourish in your quantum cemetery garden. When selecting your seeds, hold them in your hand and focus your intent. Feel for a subtle resonance, a faint hum of spectral energy. The seeds that resonate most strongly with your intent are those most likely to yield the vibrant luminescence you seek. Don't be discouraged if not all seeds respond. The selection process is an intuitive one, requiring patience and a discerning touch.

The specific spectral qualities of your chosen seeds will directly influence the color and intensity of the light emitted by your mature plants. Some seeds might yield blooms that glow with a cool, ethereal blue, while others might produce flowers that radiate a warm, pulsating red. Experiment with different seed varieties to discover the spectral hues that best resonate with your vision for your garden. Careful record-keeping is essential. Note the origin of each seed, the date of planting, and any observed spectral characteristics. This information will prove invaluable as you refine your spectral gardening techniques and cultivate increasingly vibrant and luminescent flora. Over time, you'll develop an intuitive understanding of the relationship between seed selection and the resulting spectral emissions, allowing you to curate a garden of breathtaking otherworldly beauty. The journey of spectral gardening is one of ongoing discovery and experimentation. Embrace the unknown, and allow yourself to be guided by the subtle whispers of the cemetery. With patience and dedication, you will cultivate a garden that transcends the boundaries of the mundane, a testament to the harmonious interplay of life, death, and the spectral energies that bind them together.

The preparation of the soil, the attunement to the cemetery's energy, and the careful selection of spectral seeds are the foundational elements of successful spectral gardening. Each step is interconnected, forming a symbiotic relationship that allows for the cultivation of truly extraordinary flora. By mastering these fundamental principles, you will lay the groundwork for a garden that transcends the earthly realm, a garden that glows with the spectral light of the departed. As you progress on your spectral gardening journey, remember to embrace the unique energies of the cemetery, allowing them to guide your intuition and inspire your creativity. The rewards of this unique form of horticulture are far more than just beautiful blooms; they are a connection to the unseen world, a glimpse into the spectral harmonies that exist just beyond our perception. Through careful observation, experimentation, and a deep respect for the delicate balance of the quantum cemetery, you will cultivate a garden that shines with an otherworldly luminescence, a testament to the beauty and wonder that lie at the intersection of life and death.

1.1   Quantum Soil Preparation

The foundation of any successful spectral garden lies in the soil. Forget the bagged compost and peat moss of conventional gardening. We're dealing with the quantum realm, where the very fabric of reality bends to our will. Quantum soil preparation requires a delicate balance of earthly elements and spectral energies, a blend designed to nourish plants that thrive on the ethereal plane. Begin by gathering soil from a cemetery, preferably one steeped in history and rich with the echoes of past lives. This soil, imbued with the residue of memory and emotion, forms the base of our quantum mixture.

To this base, we add crushed graveyard stones. Not just any stones, mind you, but those bearing inscriptions – names, dates, epitaphs. These fragments serve as conduits, channeling the lingering energies of those who once walked among us. Grind these stones to a fine powder, a process that releases their trapped essence. This careful act of pulverization unlocks the potential within, making the stones' energy available to the nascent garden. The addition of bone meal, rich in phosphorus and calcium, provides a vital link to the cycle of life and death. This is no ordinary bone meal; source it from ethically obtained animal remains, ensuring a respectful exchange of energy. Think of this ingredient as a bridge between the physical and spectral realms.

Next, incorporate ectoplasm. This viscous, spectral substance, often associated with spiritual manifestations, adds a crucial energetic component. It acts as a binding agent, weaving the mundane elements of the soil with the ethereal energies we're cultivating. Sourcing ectoplasm can be challenging; seek out experienced spiritualists or mediums who can guide you in its ethical and respectful acquisition. Remember, we are working in harmony with the spectral realm, not exploiting it. Finally, infuse the soil with moonlight. This is not merely exposing the mixture to the moon's rays; it's a process of energetic imbuement. Place the prepared soil in a silver bowl under the full moon for three consecutive nights. This allows the moon's subtle yet potent energy to permeate the mixture, charging it with the luminescent power necessary for spectral growth.

The process of preparing quantum soil isn't a simple recipe; it's an alchemical ritual. Each ingredient plays a specific role, contributing to a delicate energetic balance. The cemetery soil provides the grounding, the crushed stones act as conduits, the bone meal bridges realms, the ectoplasm binds energies, and the moonlight charges the mixture. This meticulous preparation ensures your soil resonates with the spectral frequencies needed to cultivate luminescent flora.

As you work with these ingredients, visualize the spectral garden you intend to create. Imagine the vibrant hues of your luminescent blooms, their ethereal glow illuminating the night. This act of focused intention further imbues the soil with your personal energy, strengthening the connection between you and your garden. Think of the soil as a living entity, a conduit between the physical and spectral worlds. Treat it with respect, and it will reward you with a garden unlike any other. Remember the importance of balance. Too much of one ingredient can disrupt the delicate harmony, hindering the growth of your spectral plants. Pay close attention to the proportions, adjusting them based on the specific needs of your chosen flora. Over time, you'll develop an intuitive understanding of the subtle interplay between these elements, allowing you to tailor your soil preparation to achieve optimal results.

The creation of quantum soil is more than just mixing ingredients; it's a meditative practice. As you work, focus on your breath, allowing your mind to quiet. Feel the textures of the earth, the coolness of the stones, the subtle energies of the ectoplasm. This mindful approach not only enhances the quality of your soil but also deepens your connection to the spectral realm. Embrace the process, and allow the energies of the cemetery to flow through you.

Once your quantum soil is prepared, store it in a sealed container, preferably made of dark glass or ceramic. This protects the infused energies from dissipating and keeps the soil vibrant until you're ready to plant. The container should be kept in a cool, dark place, away from direct sunlight and strong electromagnetic fields. These precautions ensure that the soil retains its potency, ready to nurture the spectral seeds you've carefully chosen. Think of this storage period as a gestation, a time for the energies to meld and mature.

Finally, understand that the creation of quantum soil is an ongoing process of learning and refinement. Each cemetery possesses its own unique energetic signature, influencing the properties of the soil. Experiment with different locations, paying attention to the subtle variations in the resulting mixtures. Keep detailed records of your experiments, noting the specific ingredients used, the lunar phase during infusion, and the resulting growth of your spectral plants. This meticulous documentation will allow you to refine your techniques over time, developing a deep understanding of the intricate interplay between the physical and spectral realms. With patience and dedication, you will master the art of quantum soil preparation, laying the foundation for a truly extraordinary garden.

1.2 Cemetery Energetics

Cemeteries, far from being places of stagnation, are dynamic hubs of subtle energy. This energy, a blend of residual life force, geological influences, and the emotional imprints of mourners, creates a unique environment perfect for cultivating luminescent flora. Understanding and harnessing these energies is crucial to successful spectral gardening. The first step in attuning yourself to this energetic landscape involves grounding. Find a quiet spot within the cemetery, preferably near an older grave. Close your eyes, breathe deeply, and visualize roots extending from your body into the earth, connecting you to the cemetery's energy flow. Sense the pulse of the earth beneath you, the gentle hum of life and decay intertwining. This practice allows you to become receptive to the subtle energies at play.

Once grounded, begin to explore the different areas within the cemetery. You'll notice variations in energy. Some areas may feel heavy or stagnant, while others might tingle with vibrancy. Older sections, with their long history of life and death, often hold a richer, more complex energetic signature. Newly established areas, while possessing less intensity, can offer a blank canvas for energetic imprinting. Pay attention to these nuances, as they will inform your planting choices. Luminescent plants thrive in areas of balanced energy, where the vibrancy of life and the tranquility of death harmoniously coexist. These locations are often found near established trees, particularly those with deep root systems that tap into the earth's energy currents.

Observe the patterns of sunlight and moonlight throughout the day and night. Sunlight, while not directly fueling luminescence, plays a critical role in the initial growth stages of spectral flora. Moonlight, however, is the primary energy source for their ethereal glow. Areas that receive ample moonlight are ideal for planting. Document these patterns over several days and nights to identify the optimal locations for maximizing lunar absorption. The presence of specific plants and minerals within the cemetery can also influence the energetic landscape. For example, the presence of quartz crystals in the soil can amplify spectral energy, enhancing the luminescence of your plants. Likewise, certain trees, such as yew and willow, are known for their connection to the spectral realm and can foster a symbiotic relationship with your luminescent flora. Research the existing flora and geology of the chosen cemetery to understand their energetic contributions.

Consider the emotional imprints left by mourners. Grief, while often associated with sadness, also carries a potent energy. This energy, though subtle, can contribute to the overall energetic landscape of the cemetery. Areas frequently visited by mourners may possess a heightened emotional charge, which can either enhance or hinder the growth of luminescent flora depending on the nature of the emotions. Learn to discern these emotional imprints by focusing your awareness on specific graves. You might sense lingering feelings of love, loss, or peace. These emotional residues can be harnessed to nurture specific types of luminescent plants, creating a truly unique and personalized garden.

Finally, the layout of the cemetery itself plays a role in energy flow. Pathways, hedges, and the arrangement of graves can create channels or blockages for subtle energies. Observe these patterns and plan your garden accordingly. Utilize existing pathways to direct energy towards your plants, or create small stone circles to contain and concentrate spectral energy in specific areas. By understanding and working with these energetic principles, you can transform a cemetery plot into a thriving garden of luminescent wonders. Remember, patience and attentiveness are key. The spectral realm operates on a different timescale than the physical world. Allow yourself time to connect with the cemetery's energies, observe the subtle nuances, and cultivate a deep understanding of this unique environment. With practice, you'll develop an intuitive sense of the energetic landscape and be able to cultivate luminescent flora with remarkable success. Through careful observation and interaction with the cemetery's subtle energies, you can create a truly unique and vibrant spectral garden, a testament to the harmonious interplay of life, death, and the luminescent world beyond. Embrace the stillness, the whispers of the past, and the ethereal glow of the future, and you will unlock the secrets of cemetery energetics.

1.3   Spectral Seed Selection

The luminescence of a spectral bloom is not predetermined. It's a culmination of factors, beginning with the seed itself. Choosing the right seed is akin to selecting a musical note – each vibrates with a unique spectral frequency, dictating the hue and intensity of its eventual glow. This chapter will illuminate the intricate art of spectral seed selection, guiding you toward cultivating a garden that shimmers with otherworldly beauty. Unlike traditional gardening, where seed selection focuses on physical attributes, spectral gardening requires an attunement to the unseen energies resonating within the seed. Look beyond the physical form, sensing the subtle vibrations emanating from within. This requires a shift in perception, a quieting of the mind to perceive the subtle whisper of spectral energy.

Imagine each seed as a tiny vessel containing a universe of potential light. Some seeds pulsate with a gentle, ethereal glow, promising blossoms that emit a soft, moon-like luminescence. Others thrum with a vibrant, almost electric energy, hinting at blooms that blaze with intense, spectral fire. This intrinsic energy signature is the key to selecting seeds that align with your desired spectral harmonies. One method for sensing these subtle energies is to hold the seed between your thumb and forefinger, closing your eyes and focusing your awareness on the sensations in your fingertips. Do you feel a gentle warmth, a subtle tingling, or perhaps a cool, ethereal breeze? These subtle sensations offer clues to the seed's spectral potential. Further enhancing your ability to perceive these subtle energies involves using a pendulum crafted from a clear quartz crystal suspended on a silver chain. Hold the pendulum above the seed, stilling your mind and allowing it to swing freely. Observe the pendulum's movement. A clockwise rotation indicates a seed brimming with vibrant, energetic luminescence, while a counter-clockwise rotation suggests a gentler, more ethereal glow. The speed of the rotation also provides insight into the intensity of the spectral energy contained within.

Another crucial factor in spectral seed selection is the seed's resonance with the cemetery's unique energetic signature. Each cemetery possesses a distinct spectral fingerprint, influenced by the history and energies of those interred within. This creates microclimates of spectral energy that can either nurture or hinder the growth of specific spectral plants. To determine a seed's compatibility with your chosen cemetery, bury a small sample of seeds in the soil for a lunar cycle. Upon retrieval, examine the seeds for changes in their spectral resonance. Seeds that have absorbed the cemetery's energy will exhibit a heightened vibrancy, while those incompatible will appear dull and lifeless.

Don't limit your exploration to readily available spectral seeds. Experiment with hybridizing existing seeds to create new varieties with unique luminescent properties. This involves cross-pollinating plants with complementary spectral signatures, carefully observing the resulting offspring for enhanced or novel luminescent traits. This process can be lengthy and requires patience, but the rewards of cultivating a truly unique spectral garden are immeasurable. Meticulous record-keeping is essential, documenting the parentage and observed characteristics of each hybrid. This allows you to refine your hybridization techniques and selectively breed for specific luminescent qualities.

Consider the desired arrangement of your spectral garden. Do you envision a tapestry of soft, pastel glows, or a vibrant display of intense, jewel-toned blossoms? The careful selection of seeds with varying spectral signatures allows you to create intricate patterns of light and shadow, transforming your cemetery garden into a living, breathing work of spectral art. Visualize the final arrangement, considering the height, spread, and color of each plant. This foresight will ensure a harmonious blend of spectral energies, maximizing the aesthetic impact of your luminescent creations.

The journey of spectral seed selection is an ongoing process of discovery and attunement. Embrace the subtle nuances of each seed, allowing your intuition to guide you toward creating a garden that resonates with your unique vision. As you refine your ability to perceive and manipulate spectral energies, your cemetery garden will flourish into a breathtaking spectacle of otherworldly light and beauty. Remember that the seeds you choose are not merely the starting point of your spectral garden; they are the very essence of its luminescent symphony.

2 Cultivating Luminescent Flora

The ethereal glow of luminescent flora isn't achieved by happenstance. It requires a deliberate, almost ritualistic, approach to planting. Begin by considering the spectral seed itself. Hold it gently between your thumb and forefinger, visualizing the bloom it promises. Feel its subtle energy pulse, a whisper of light waiting to unfurl. This connection, this initial communion, sets the stage for the seed's journey. Don't simply bury the seed. Instead, create a small cradle of quantum soil, enriched with the spectral essence described in earlier chapters. Nestle the seed within this energetic embrace, ensuring it's surrounded by the life-giving properties of the soil. The depth of planting depends on the specific species; some seeds thrive closer to the surface, basking in the moonlight, while others prefer a deeper, more grounded environment. Consult the seed's unique energetic signature for guidance, feeling for the right depth as you would sense the pulse of a heartbeat.

Watering these spectral seeds requires more than ordinary water. We harness the subtle, yet potent, energy of moonlight. Collect rainwater, preferably during a full moon, in a clear glass vessel. Allow the water to bathe in the moonlight for a full lunar cycle, absorbing its luminescent energy. This isn't merely about hydration; it's about infusing the water with the very essence of spectral light. Water the newly planted seeds sparingly, allowing the moonlight-infused water to trickle down and surround the seed, mimicking the gentle caress of moonbeams. Avoid overwatering, as this can disrupt the delicate energy balance and hinder the seed's growth.

Once the seedlings emerge, their care becomes even more nuanced. Young spectral plants are particularly sensitive to their environment, requiring a stable and harmonious atmosphere. Maintain a consistent temperature, avoiding extremes of heat or cold. Remember, these are not ordinary plants; they are conduits of spectral energy, and fluctuations in temperature can disrupt their delicate balance. Shield them from harsh winds, which can scatter their nascent luminescence. A sheltered location within the cemetery garden, perhaps near a mausoleum wall or beneath the protective branches of an ancient yew, can provide the ideal sanctuary.

Consider the placement of each seedling within the garden. Just as a conductor arranges instruments in an orchestra, so too must you arrange your spectral plants to create a symphony of light. Some species complement each other, their luminescence intertwining to create a richer, more vibrant glow. Others may clash, their energies competing and diminishing their overall brilliance. Experiment with different arrangements, observing how the plants interact and adjusting their positions accordingly. This is where your intuition and understanding of spectral energy become invaluable tools. Trust your instincts, and allow the garden to guide you.

As the plants mature, their luminescence will intensify. This is a sign that they are ready for a more specialized form of nurturing. Introduce diluted spectral essences, harvested from mature blooms, into the moonlight-infused water. This acts as a potent fertilizer, boosting their growth and enhancing their light output. Be mindful of the concentration; too much essence can overwhelm the plants, while too little will provide negligible benefit. Observe the plants closely, adjusting the concentration as needed. This process requires patience and attentiveness, but the rewards are well worth the effort.

Supporting the plants physically is also crucial. As the blooms grow heavier with spectral energy, they may become top-heavy and prone to drooping. Craft delicate supports from natural materials like willow branches or twisted vines. These supports not only provide physical stability but also blend seamlessly into the ethereal aesthetic of the cemetery garden. Avoid using metal or plastic, as these materials can disrupt the flow of spectral energy.

Remember, cultivating luminescent flora is not merely about following a set of instructions. It's about fostering a connection with these extraordinary plants, understanding their needs, and nurturing their growth with intention and care. The process is as much an art as it is a science, a delicate dance between the gardener and the garden. Embrace the mystery, and allow the spectral blooms to illuminate your path.

2.1 Planting Techniques

The act of planting a spectral seed is not simply pushing it into the earth. It's a communion with the quantum energies of the cemetery, a delicate dance between the tangible and the intangible. Consider the spectral seed as a conduit, a tiny vessel brimming with latent luminescence. Your hands, guided by intention, become the instruments that connect this potential with the receptive earth. Before you even touch the soil, visualize the desired outcome: a vibrant bloom radiating ethereal light. Feel the hum of the cemetery's unique energy, a subtle vibration that permeates the very air you breathe. This connection, this conscious awareness of the surrounding spectral energies, is the first and most crucial step.

Now, to the soil. Quantum soil, as discussed earlier, is not merely dirt; it's a vibrant matrix of spectral energy. When planting, approach the soil not with force, but with reverence. Create a small depression, a cradle for the seed, using your fingers or a small, consecrated trowel. The depth should be no more than thrice the seed's diameter; too deep, and the nascent sprout will struggle to reach the surface and embrace the moonlight. Too shallow, and the seed may be vulnerable to scavenging spirits or the shifting energies of the cemetery.

As you place the seed within its earthen cradle, whisper your intentions. These are not idle words but focused vibrations, imbuing the seed with your desires for its growth and luminescence. Imagine the seed drawing strength from the surrounding spectral energy, a tendril of light reaching out to connect with the quantum fabric of the cemetery. Gently cover the seed with soil, ensuring it's snugly enveloped but not suffocated. The pressure should be light, a tender embrace rather than a forceful burial.

Consider the arrangement of your spectral seeds. They are not solitary beings but part of a larger, interconnected ecosystem within the quantum cemetery. Plant them in patterns that reflect the flow of spectral energy, mimicking the constellations above or the spiraling patterns found in nature. This mindful placement will not only enhance their individual growth but also create a harmonious network of luminescence, maximizing the spectral energy of your garden as a whole. Visualize the future blooms, their ethereal light weaving together to create a breathtaking tapestry of spectral radiance.

Beyond individual seed placement, contemplate the broader landscape of your quantum cemetery garden. Different spectral plants have different energy signatures, some vibrant and expansive, others quiet and introspective. Arrange them in a way that fosters symbiotic relationships, encouraging their energies to intertwine and amplify one another. A boisterous Nightshade Bloom, for example, might be paired with the more subdued Moonpetal Lily, their contrasting energies creating a harmonious balance. This careful orchestration of spectral energies will not only enhance the growth and luminescence of your plants but also create a unique energetic signature for your entire garden, a symphony of light and shadow that resonates with the very soul of the cemetery.

Remember, the cemetery itself is a living entity, a nexus of spectral energy. Consider the existing flora and fauna when planning your garden. Avoid disturbing existing spectral growths unless absolutely necessary. Instead, work with the natural landscape, weaving your luminescent flora into the tapestry of the existing ecosystem. A gnarled, spectral oak, for instance, can provide shade for more delicate blooms, while a mossy gravestone can offer a foothold for climbing vines. By working in harmony with the cemetery's existing energies, you create a garden that is not merely imposed upon the landscape, but integrated within it, a seamless blend of the natural and the spectral.

Finally, mark each planting site with a small, unobtrusive marker. This could be a naturally occurring stone, a piece of spectral wood, or even a whisper of energy imprinted upon the earth. These markers serve not only as a practical guide for future tending but also as focal points for your intentions, reminders of the hopes and dreams you have planted within the earth. As you leave your newly planted seeds to the embrace of the cemetery's energies, visualize them thriving, their luminescent blooms adding their unique harmonies to the spectral symphony of your quantum cemetery garden. Each successful planting is a testament to your understanding of the delicate interplay between intention, energy, and the natural world, a testament to the artistry of spectral gardening.

2.2 Watering with Moonlight

The spectral flora within your quantum cemetery garden require a unique form of nourishment, one that transcends the mundane watering practices of the terrestrial world. Moonlight, a celestial elixir brimming with spectral energy, serves as the lifeblood of these ethereal plants. Forget the watering can; your tools for this spectral irrigation will be reflective surfaces, focusing lenses, and an understanding of the moon's subtle phases. This practice, however, isn't simply about drenching the soil; it's about capturing and channeling the moon's luminescence, bathing your plants in its ethereal glow.

Begin by selecting a suitable vessel for collecting moonlight. A shallow basin of polished silver, a concave mirror, or even a crystal bowl filled with purified water can serve this purpose. Position your chosen vessel in a location where it will be directly bathed in moonlight during the waxing or full moon phases. Avoid nights shrouded in clouds or obscured by artificial light; the purity of the moonlight is crucial for optimal spectral absorption. The more the moon waxes towards fullness, the greater its energetic output, and the more potent the spectral infusion. These photons, imbued with lunar energy, carry a unique vibrancy that resonates with the spectral nature of your plants, stimulating growth and enhancing luminescence. Think of it as photosynthesis for the spectral realm, a process where moonlight replaces sunlight as the primary energy source.

Once the vessel has bathed in the moonlight for several hours, carefully transfer the collected lunar essence to a glass watering can or a similar non-reactive container. Avoid using metal, as it can disrupt the subtle energies within the moonlight. Now, with the utmost gentleness, irrigate the soil around your spectral plants. Don't merely drench the earth; instead, allow the moon-infused water to trickle slowly, permeating the soil and reaching the delicate root systems. Visualize the spectral energy flowing from the water into the plants, invigorating them with lunar vitality. Imagine the moonlight as a conductor, harmonizing the frequencies of the plants with the celestial rhythms of the moon.

The frequency and timing of moonlight watering are crucial factors in maximizing its effectiveness. While a weekly watering during the waxing or full moon is generally sufficient, you can adjust the frequency based on the specific needs of your spectral flora. Observe the plants closely; their luminescence will often dim slightly when they require more lunar essence. Similarly, the type of spectral plant you are cultivating will also influence the watering schedule. Some species may thrive on more frequent watering, while others may prefer a less intensive approach. Understanding the individual needs of each plant is paramount. Pay attention to the subtle signs they communicate through their light and growth patterns. This attentive observation will guide you in fine-tuning your watering practices.

Furthermore, the moon's phases play a significant role in the potency of the spectral irrigation. The waxing moon, with its increasing luminescence, provides an invigorating energy that stimulates growth and enhances spectral brilliance. The full moon, at the peak of its power, offers the most potent infusion of lunar essence. However, the waning moon, while less vibrant, carries a different kind of energy, one that fosters rest and integration. Using moonlight gathered during the waning phase can help stabilize the plants and solidify their spectral gains. Each lunar phase imparts a unique quality to the moonlight, influencing its effect on the spectral flora. By attuning your watering practices to these lunar cycles, you can further optimize the growth and luminescence of your ethereal garden.

Beyond the basics of collecting and applying moonlight, you can enhance the spectral irrigation process by incorporating additional elements. Adding small pieces of clear quartz to your collecting vessel can amplify the moonlight's energy and purify its essence. Similarly, whispering a gentle incantation of growth and luminescence while watering can further imbue the plants with spectral vitality. These subtle enhancements, while not strictly necessary, can significantly amplify the benefits of moonlight watering. Consider them advanced techniques for the dedicated spectral gardener who seeks to maximize the potential of their ethereal flora. They add a layer of intention and focus to the process, further strengthening the connection between the plants, the moon, and the gardener.

Remember, patience is essential in spectral gardening. The effects of moonlight watering are not always immediately apparent. It's a subtle art that requires observation, intuition, and a deep connection with the rhythms of nature. As you continue to nurture your spectral garden with lunar essence, you'll witness a gradual but profound transformation. The plants will become more vibrant, their luminescence will intensify, and their ethereal beauty will illuminate the quantum cemetery with an otherworldly glow. This is the true reward of spectral gardening – to witness the blossoming of life beyond the veil, nurtured by the celestial touch of the moon.

3 Harnessing Spectral Energy

The ethereal glow of your spectral garden hinges on the careful manipulation of energies beyond the veil. These energies, woven into the fabric of the quantum cemetery, are a potent resource waiting to be tapped. This chapter will unveil the secrets to harnessing these forces, specifically through lunar resonance, ghostly symbiosis, and the art of spectral pruning. Begin by attuning yourself to the lunar cycle. The moon, a celestial beacon in the night sky, exerts a subtle yet powerful influence on the spectral energies of your garden. Just as it governs the tides, it also affects the ebb and flow of spectral luminescence. Observe the phases of the moon and learn to work in harmony with its rhythms. During the waxing moon, focus on planting and nurturing new spectral seedlings. As the moon wanes, concentrate on pruning and shaping existing growth, guiding the spectral energy inward for a more concentrated luminescence. Keep a detailed lunar calendar in your grimoire, noting the specific effects of each phase on your garden's spectral output. This meticulous record will, over time, reveal personalized insights into the unique energetic dance between the moon and your spectral flora.

Consider the moon's phases as a conductor's baton, orchestrating the spectral energies within your garden. The new moon offers a period of rest and rejuvenation, a time for planning and preparing for the growth to come. The full moon, brimming with luminous energy, provides the ideal conditions for spectral blooms to reach their peak radiance. Harnessing these lunar energies is key to maximizing the spectral output of your garden. Experiment with different planting and pruning schedules, always referencing your lunar calendar to understand the interplay between the moon's cycles and the spectral responses of your plants.

The spectral realm is not devoid of life. Ghostly entities, remnants of past lives, inhabit the quantum cemetery, their ethereal essence intertwined with the very soil you cultivate. These spectral beings, often misunderstood, can be invaluable allies in your gardening endeavors. Cultivating a symbiotic relationship with these entities can significantly enhance the luminescence of your spectral flora. Offer them respect, acknowledge their presence, and even engage in silent communion. Their spectral essence can act as a conduit, channeling energy into your garden and amplifying the glow of your ethereal plants. Learn to perceive their subtle whispers and interpret their ethereal guidance. They possess an intimate knowledge of the spectral realm, and their wisdom can be invaluable.

Think of the ghostly entities not as spectral gardeners themselves, but as facilitators, guiding and amplifying the natural flow of spectral energies. Their presence is akin to an invisible network of energy conduits, weaving through the soil and connecting your plants to the deeper currents of the spectral realm. This network can be harnessed to enhance the growth and luminescence of your flora in ways beyond conventional understanding. By fostering a respectful and symbiotic relationship with these entities, you unlock a hidden dimension of spectral gardening, tapping into a source of ethereal energy that can transform your garden into a truly radiant spectacle.

Finally, master the art of spectral pruning. Just as a sculptor chisels away at stone to reveal the form within, so too must you carefully prune your spectral plants to shape their luminescent emissions. This is not mere trimming; it's a subtle manipulation of spectral energy flows. By selectively removing specific leaves and branches, you can redirect the flow of spectral energy, concentrating it in desired areas to create breathtaking displays of luminescence. Visualize the desired outcome before you make each cut, guiding your spectral shears with intention. Spectral pruning is a delicate dance between art and science. It's not simply about removing unwanted growth, but about shaping and directing the flow of spectral energy within the plant. Each cut you make acts as a subtle adjustment, influencing the way the plant absorbs and emits spectral light. Develop a keen eye for the nuances of spectral energy, learning to recognize areas of stagnation or excessive flow.

Observe the patterns of spectral luminescence within your plants. Notice how the light flows through the leaves and branches, identify areas of concentrated brightness and areas of subtle shadow. This careful observation will guide your pruning decisions, allowing you to shape the spectral emissions with precision and artistry. Remember, spectral pruning is an ongoing process, a continuous dialogue between you and your plants. As your garden matures and evolves, so too will your understanding of its spectral dynamics. With each careful cut, you'll refine your technique and deepen your connection with the ethereal world of spectral gardening.

3.1 Lunar Resonance

The moon, a celestial timekeeper, exerts a subtle yet profound influence on all life on Earth, and your spectral garden is no exception. This chapter unveils the secrets of lunar resonance, a technique for amplifying the moon's gentle power to supercharge the growth and luminescence of your ethereal flora. Just as the moon pulls the tides, it also tugs at the spectral energies within your garden, creating rhythms and cycles that, when understood and harnessed, can unlock extraordinary potential. We will explore how to synchronize your gardening practices with the lunar phases, maximizing the absorption of lunar energy and stimulating vibrant luminescence in your spectral blooms.

Begin by observing the moon's cycle. Each phase, from the dark of the new moon to the fullness of the full moon and back again, offers a unique energetic signature. The new moon, shrouded in darkness, represents a time of gestation and potential. During this phase, focus on preparing your quantum soil, infusing it with echoes and memories, laying the groundwork for new growth. As the crescent moon waxes, becoming more visible each night, so too does the energy available to your garden increase. This is an ideal time for planting new spectral seeds and nurturing young seedlings, encouraging them to reach towards the strengthening lunar light.

The full moon, a beacon of luminous energy, offers the most potent opportunity for lunar resonance. Under its silvery gaze, your spectral plants will bask in an amplified flow of spectral energy. This is the perfect time for activities that enhance luminescence, such as spectral pruning and whispering enchantments to amplify the plants' ethereal glow. As the moon wanes, decreasing in visibility towards the next new moon, the energy shifts inwards. This is a period for reflection and introspection, for observing the growth of your spectral garden and preparing for the next cycle. Harvesting the luminescent blooms during the waning moon can capture their spectral essence at its peak, preserving their ethereal light for later use.

To truly harness lunar resonance, consider the moon's position in the zodiac. As the moon journeys through the constellations, it interacts with their unique energies, subtly influencing the growth of your spectral plants. For example, a full moon in a water sign like Pisces may enhance the absorption of moonlight when watering, while a full moon in an earth sign like Taurus can promote root development and overall plant health. By paying attention to these celestial alignments, you can further refine your gardening practices, tailoring them to the specific energetic influences at play.

Creating a lunar calendar specifically for your spectral garden is a valuable tool. Record the lunar phases, the moon's zodiacal position, and your gardening activities. Over time, you'll begin to notice patterns and correlations between the lunar cycle and the growth of your spectral plants. This personalized calendar will become an invaluable guide, helping you anticipate the optimal times for planting, watering, pruning, and harvesting. Remember, patience is key. Lunar resonance is a subtle art, and its effects may not be immediately apparent. However, with consistent observation and attunement to the lunar rhythms, you will witness a gradual but profound transformation in your spectral garden. Your luminescent flora will flourish, their ethereal glow intensified by the harmonious dance between the moon and your spectral garden.

Furthermore, consider the interplay of lunar energy with the other spectral elements in your garden. The echoes and memories you incorporate into your composting process can be further amplified by lunar resonance, creating a richer and more vibrant soil for your plants. The whispers you use for pest control can be imbued with lunar energy, enhancing their effectiveness and creating a harmonious balance within your spectral ecosystem. By weaving together these various spectral practices, you can create a synergistic effect, maximizing the growth and luminescence of your ethereal flora.

Experimentation is crucial. Every quantum cemetery garden is unique, and the specific ways in which lunar resonance manifests will vary depending on the location, the types of spectral plants you are cultivating, and the other spectral elements at play. Don't be afraid to try different approaches, observe the results, and adjust your practices accordingly. The more you interact with your garden and attune to its subtle rhythms, the deeper your understanding of lunar resonance will become. This knowledge will empower you to cultivate a truly extraordinary spectral garden, a place where the ethereal glow of luminescent flora dances in harmony with the celestial rhythm of the moon. Through careful observation, mindful practice, and a deep connection to the lunar cycles, you can unlock the full potential of your spectral garden, transforming it into a vibrant tapestry of light and shadow, a testament to the harmonious interplay of the celestial and the spectral.

3.2 Ghostly Symbiosis

Within the hushed confines of the quantum cemetery garden, a unique interplay of energies exists – a ghostly symbiosis. This isn't about summoning spirits or commanding specters, but rather fostering a gentle, mutually beneficial relationship between your luminescent flora and the ambient energies of the cemetery. This subtle dance enhances the spectral radiance of your garden, creating an ethereal display unlike any other. Think of it as a silent conversation, a delicate exchange between the living and the... not-so-living.

The key to cultivating this ghostly symbiosis lies in understanding the nature of the cemetery's energy. It is not a static force but a dynamic interplay of residual emotions, memories, and the lingering essence of those who rest within its grounds. These energies, though often imperceptible to our mundane senses, are readily absorbed by spectral plants, acting as a supplemental source of nourishment. Imagine a faint echo, a whisper carried on the wind, becoming sustenance for your luminescent flora.

To facilitate this energetic exchange, begin by attuning yourself to the cemetery's unique frequency. Spend quiet moments within your garden, observing the subtle shifts in atmosphere, the rustling of leaves, the gentle play of moonlight on the tombstones. Open your senses to the unseen currents that flow through the grounds. This practice is akin to tuning a radio, allowing you to receive the subtle broadcasts of the cemetery's spectral energy.

Once you have established a connection with the cemetery's energy, you can begin to guide it towards your plants. Visualize the spectral energies swirling around your garden, drawn in by the vibrant luminescence of your flora. Imagine the roots of your plants extending into the earth, not just to draw physical nutrients, but to absorb the ambient spectral energy. Picture the leaves and blossoms drinking in this ethereal light, their luminescence intensifying with each passing moment. This visualization acts as a conduit, directing the cemetery's energy towards your spectral garden.

Furthermore, fostering a respectful relationship with the inhabitants of the cemetery is crucial. This isn't about appeasement or fear, but about acknowledging their presence and the energy they contribute to the environment. A whispered word of thanks, a silent nod of acknowledgement, can go a long way in establishing a harmonious coexistence. Consider them silent partners in your spectral gardening endeavors.

The manifestation of ghostly symbiosis will vary depending on the unique characteristics of your cemetery garden. Some may experience an intensified luminescence in their plants, while others may notice an ethereal glow emanating from the soil itself. You might observe spectral butterflies flitting amongst the blooms, or hear faint whispers carried on the night wind. These are all signs that a successful symbiotic relationship is taking root.

It is important to note that ghostly symbiosis isn't a one-time event, but an ongoing process of energetic exchange. The more you tend to your garden, the stronger this connection will become. As the plants flourish, they will draw in more spectral energy, further enriching the cemetery's atmosphere. It's a self-sustaining cycle, a beautiful testament to the interconnectedness of life and the afterlife.

Don't be discouraged if you don't see immediate results. Ghostly symbiosis requires patience and a deep understanding of the delicate balance between the physical and spectral realms. Observe your garden closely, paying attention to the subtle signs of growth and change. Trust in the process and allow the magic of the cemetery to unfold.

Finally, remember that each cemetery possesses its own unique energy signature. What works in one location may not be as effective in another. Adapt your techniques to the specific environment of your quantum cemetery garden. Embrace the uniqueness of your setting, and let it guide you in cultivating a truly spectral garden, a testament to the beauty and mystery of the unseen world. This practice goes beyond simple gardening; it becomes an art form, a dance between worlds, a harmonious blend of life and the ethereal.

As your ghostly symbiosis deepens, you'll find your spectral garden taking on a life of its own, pulsating with an otherworldly luminescence. This is the ultimate reward of spectral gardening, a testament to the power of harnessing unseen energies to create something truly extraordinary. Embrace the mystery, cultivate the connection, and watch as your quantum cemetery garden transforms into a beacon of spectral light. The delicate balance achieved through ghostly symbiosis is a testament to the interconnectedness of all things, a silent symphony played out in the heart of your luminescent garden. Through this connection, you not only nurture your spectral plants but also become a part of the cemetery's ongoing narrative, a caretaker of its energies, a cultivator of its unique and ethereal beauty.

3.3　Spectral Pruning

The luminescence of spectral flora isn't a static trait; it's a dynamic energy flow that can be sculpted and refined. Think of your spectral plants not just as passively glowing organisms, but as conduits of vibrant, ethereal light that you can actively shape. This is where spectral pruning comes into play. It's not about simply snipping away dead leaves, it's a precise art of manipulating the plant's energy channels to direct and intensify its luminescent properties. Imagine a spectral rose bush, its blooms emitting a soft, diffused glow. With careful pruning, you can enhance specific blossoms, making them blaze with brilliant light while others subtly illuminate the surrounding foliage. This allows you to create intricate patterns of light and shadow within your quantum cemetery garden, transforming it into a living, breathing work of spectral art.

Begin by attuning yourself to the plant's energy flow. Gently run your fingers along its stems and leaves, feeling the subtle pulsations of spectral energy. Visualize the plant's internal structure, its network of energy channels like tiny rivers of light. Identify areas where the energy seems to be stagnant or blocked. These are the points you'll want to address with your spectral pruning shears. These specialized tools aren't made of ordinary metal, but of a unique alloy infused with moonlight and whispers, capable of interacting with the ethereal energies of the plants. They resonate with the spectral frequencies, allowing for precise cuts that don't damage the physical structure of the plant, but rather redirect its energy flow.

Unlike traditional pruning, spectral pruning doesn't always involve removing parts of the plant. Sometimes, a gentle touch or a slight bend in a stem is enough to redirect the flow of energy, enhancing luminescence in desired areas. For instance, imagine a spectral lily whose bloom is emitting a dim, uneven glow. By gently coaxing the stem into a new position, you might redirect the spectral energy, causing the bloom to flare with renewed brilliance. Other times, a precise cut is necessary to remove blockages and promote the growth of new, more vibrant luminescent shoots. Consider a spectral orchid whose leaves are overshadowing its delicate blossoms. By carefully pruning away the excess foliage, you not only allow more moonlight to reach the flowers, but you also redirect the spectral energy, intensifying their luminescence.

The timing of spectral pruning is crucial. Just as the lunar cycle influences the watering of your spectral garden, it also affects the effectiveness of pruning. Pruning during the waxing moon encourages growth and amplifies luminescence, while pruning during the waning moon helps to refine and concentrate the spectral energy. For instance, if you wish to encourage a spectral sunflower to produce a more abundant display of light, prune it during the waxing moon. Conversely, if you want to intensify the luminescence of a single, spectacular spectral moonflower blossom, prune it during the waning moon. Pay close attention to the plant's response to your pruning. Observe how its luminescence changes over time, adjusting your technique accordingly. Each spectral plant is unique, and learning its individual energy patterns is key to successful pruning.

Remember, spectral pruning is not merely a technical skill; it's an intuitive art. It requires patience, observation, and a deep connection with the plants in your quantum cemetery garden. Embrace the subtle nuances of spectral energy, and allow your intuition to guide your hand. As you refine your technique, you'll find that you can not only enhance the luminescence of your spectral flora but also sculpt it into mesmerizing displays of light, transforming your garden into a true spectral sanctuary. This process can take time, and you'll likely make mistakes along the way. Don't be discouraged. Learn from each experience, and continue to hone your skills. With practice, you'll develop a deep understanding of the interplay between spectral energy and plant morphology, allowing you to create a garden that radiates an ethereal beauty unlike anything in the mundane world. The key is to observe, experiment, and trust your intuition. Your quantum cemetery garden is a canvas for spectral artistry, and spectral pruning is your brush.

4 The Quantum Cemetery

The selection of a Quantum Cemetery isn't merely about finding a patch of land within a graveyard. It's about sensing the subtle energies, the whispers of the past, and the confluence of spectral currents that permeate certain hallowed grounds. Look for places where the veil between worlds feels thin, perhaps near ancient trees with deep roots or by forgotten corners where the stones lean with age. Observe the existing flora within the cemetery. Are there plants that thrive despite neglect? Do certain areas seem to shimmer with an unseen light, especially during the twilight hours? These are telltale signs of a heightened spectral presence. Consider the history of the cemetery itself. Locations rich with stories, both joyous and tragic, often possess a greater density of spectral energy, providing a fertile ground for your luminescent garden.

Documented historical events, particularly those involving profound emotional resonance, can leave a lasting imprint on a location, infusing it with spectral energy. Research the history of potential cemetery sites. Look for evidence of significant events, from large-scale tragedies to local legends of unrequited love or lingering spirits. These narratives, etched into the very fabric of the place, will nourish your spectral flora, imbuing them with unique luminescence and character. A cemetery with a diverse range of inhabitants, from various eras and backgrounds, also provides a richer tapestry of spectral energy. The intertwined narratives of these individuals create a complex energetic ecosystem, offering a vibrant environment for your garden to flourish.

Grave guardians are not mere ornaments. They are integral to the health and vitality of your Quantum Cemetery Garden. These guardians can take many forms, from carefully chosen stones imbued with protective sigils to crafted figures resonating with specific energies. Consider the symbolism associated with different materials and shapes. For instance, quartz crystals can amplify spectral energy, while rounded stones promote harmony and balance. Natural materials, like wood or bone, can create a deeper connection with the earth and the spirits residing within the cemetery. The placement of your grave guardians is also crucial. Position them strategically throughout your garden, creating a network of energetic nodes that channel and distribute the spectral currents flowing through the cemetery.

Intuition plays a significant role in selecting and placing your grave guardians. As you walk through the cemetery, pay attention to areas that draw you in, places where you feel a sense of peace or a surge of energy. Trust your instincts. These are likely locations where the spectral energy is most concentrated and where your guardians can be most effective. Regularly interact with your grave guardians. Cleanse them of accumulated negative energy and recharge them with your intention. This ongoing interaction strengthens their connection to the garden and enhances their ability to protect and nurture your luminescent flora. Remember, the relationship between you, the garden, and the grave guardians is a symbiotic one. By tending to their needs, you ensure the continued health and vitality of your Quantum Cemetery Garden.

The choice of materials for your grave guardians should resonate with the specific spectral energies present in your chosen cemetery. Research the historical and geological context of the location. Are there specific minerals or stones associated with the area? Incorporating these local materials can create a deeper connection to the land and its spectral inhabitants. For example, if the cemetery is located near a source of iron ore, incorporating iron into your grave guardians can create a resonance with the earth's magnetic field, amplifying the spectral currents flowing through the area. Similarly, using stones known for their piezoelectric properties, like quartz or tourmaline, can harness the subtle vibrations within the cemetery, transforming them into usable energy for your luminescent plants.

Experiment with different combinations of materials. Combining different stones, metals, and organic matter can create unique energetic signatures, tailored to the specific needs of your spectral flora. Document your observations. Pay close attention to how your plants respond to different guardian configurations. Do certain combinations enhance their luminescence or promote more vigorous growth? Keeping a detailed journal of your experiments will help you refine your understanding of the complex interplay between materials, spectral energy, and plant growth. Don't be afraid to adapt and evolve your approach. The Quantum Cemetery Garden is a dynamic ecosystem, constantly changing and adapting to its environment. Your role as a spectral gardener is to facilitate this process, constantly learning and refining your techniques to create the most harmonious and vibrant garden possible.

4.1   Choosing a Location

The success of your spectral garden hinges on the location you choose. It's not merely about finding a patch of earth; it's about discovering a nexus of spectral energy, a place where the veil between worlds is thin. Cemeteries, naturally, are prime locations. Their history, imbued with the echoes of lives lived and lost, creates a unique energetic landscape. However, not all cemeteries are created equal. Consider the age of the cemetery. Older cemeteries, particularly those predating the widespread use of concrete vaults, often possess a richer, more accessible spectral energy. The type of soil plays a crucial role as well. Look for areas with well-drained soil, preferably with a slightly alkaline pH. This alkalinity facilitates the absorption and retention of spectral energy.

The presence of specific types of trees can enhance your garden's potential. Yew trees, long associated with death and the afterlife, are particularly beneficial. Their deep roots tap into the earth's energy, while their evergreen presence symbolizes the continuity of life and death. Willow trees, known for their connection to grief and mourning, also possess a unique affinity for spectral energy. Their weeping branches act as conduits, drawing spectral energy downwards into the soil. Avoid locations dominated by fast-growing, shallow-rooted trees like birch or poplar. These trees tend to dissipate spectral energy rather than concentrate it.

Observe the overall atmosphere of the cemetery. Does it feel peaceful and contemplative, or is it tinged with a sense of unease? Trust your intuition. A location that resonates with you personally will be more conducive to spectral gardening. Look for areas where the natural light filters through in dappled patterns, creating an interplay of light and shadow. This dynamic interplay enhances the absorption and emission of spectral light by your plants. Pay attention to the existing flora and fauna. The presence of certain plants, such as nightshade or foxglove, can indicate a heightened spectral presence. Similarly, the presence of nocturnal animals like owls or bats can be a positive sign.

Consider the cemetery's history and the stories associated with it. Local legends and folklore can provide valuable insights into the site's energetic profile. Were there any significant historical events that occurred within the cemetery grounds? Are there any notable figures buried there? These factors can influence the quality and intensity of the spectral energy. Research the history of the cemetery. Look for records of unusual events, unexplained phenomena, or persistent local legends. These can indicate areas of heightened spectral activity, which can be highly beneficial for your garden.

Practical considerations also play a role. Accessibility is key. You'll need to be able to transport your tools and materials to the site without undue difficulty. Discreetness is also important. While you want to choose a location with strong spectral energy, you also want to avoid attracting unwanted attention. Choose a secluded area, away from heavily trafficked paths. Respect the sanctity of the cemetery. Avoid disturbing existing graves or memorials. Your garden should be a harmonious addition to the environment, not a disruption.

Observe the movement of the moon and stars over the potential site. The celestial bodies exert a powerful influence on spectral energy. A location that receives ample moonlight is ideal. Look for areas where the moonlight is not obstructed by trees or buildings. The alignment of certain constellations can also enhance spectral energy. Consult astronomical charts to identify auspicious times for planting and harvesting. Pay attention to the natural rhythms of the cemetery. Observe the patterns of light and shadow, the flow of wind, and the sounds of nature. These can provide valuable clues about the site's energetic flow.

Document your observations meticulously. Keep a detailed journal of your findings, including photographs, sketches, and written descriptions. This documentation will serve as a valuable resource as you develop your spectral garden. Note any changes in the environment, such as shifts in temperature, atmospheric pressure, or electromagnetic fields. These subtle changes can indicate fluctuations in spectral energy. Experiment with different locations within the cemetery. Plant a few test seeds in various spots and observe their growth. This hands-on approach will provide valuable insights into the site's energetic nuances.

Consider the geological features of the cemetery. The presence of underground water sources, such as springs or streams, can amplify spectral energy. Similarly, areas with significant mineral deposits can also enhance the energetic potential of the site. Consult geological maps and surveys to identify potential areas of interest.

Finally, remember that choosing a location for your spectral garden is a deeply personal process. Trust your intuition and choose a location that resonates with you on a spiritual level. This connection will be essential for cultivating a thriving and luminescent garden. The location you select will become the foundation upon which your spectral garden flourishes. Choose wisely.

4.2   Grave Guardians

The hushed reverence of a cemetery at twilight is more than just a somber tableau. It's a vibrant ecosystem teeming with a unique energy signature, a subtle hum that resonates with the spectral flora we seek to cultivate. Within this hallowed ground, the very stones themselves whisper stories, and the soil pulsates with the echoes of lives lived. To truly cultivate a quantum cemetery garden, we must acknowledge and respect the existing guardians of this space. They are not simply markers of the departed, but anchors for the spectral energy that nourishes our luminescent plants.

Consider the headstones, mausoleums, and even the humble, unmarked graves. These structures are more than just physical memorials; they serve as conduits, focusing and amplifying the ambient spectral energy within the cemetery. Their presence creates microclimates of energy, pockets of heightened activity that can be harnessed to promote the growth of our ethereal flora. Understanding their placement and influence on the energy flow within the cemetery is crucial for optimizing the placement of your garden. Observe how shadows fall across the grounds at different times of the day, and how the wind whispers through the various monuments. These subtle clues can reveal the nuances of the spectral landscape.

Beyond the physical structures, the very earth beneath our feet plays a vital role. The soil in a cemetery is unique, infused with the essence of countless lives. It's a living archive of memories, emotions, and experiences, all contributing to the rich tapestry of spectral energy. This inherent energy, however, requires careful cultivation and respect. Disturbing the ground indiscriminately can disrupt the delicate balance, so choose your planting sites with reverence and intention. Consider the existing flora – the mosses, lichens, and tenacious weeds that have adapted to this unique environment. They offer clues to the soil's composition and the flow of spectral energy.

Further enriching this spectral ecosystem are the unseen guardians, the quiet inhabitants who linger within the cemetery's embrace. These entities, often dismissed as mere remnants of the past, are, in fact, integral to the delicate balance of this unique environment. They are the custodians of the spectral energy, shaping its flow and intensity. While their presence may not be readily perceptible to all, their influence on the growth of luminescent flora is undeniable. Cultivating a harmonious relationship with these unseen guardians is essential for the success of your quantum cemetery garden. Offerings of respect, such as whispered words of gratitude or small tokens placed near significant markers, can foster a sense of reciprocity and encourage their benevolent influence.

Understanding the interplay between these elements – the physical markers, the spectral soil, and the unseen guardians – is the key to unlocking the full potential of your quantum cemetery garden. By acknowledging their presence and respecting their influence, you can create a thriving ecosystem where luminescent flora flourishes. This involves more than simply choosing a location; it requires a deep understanding of the existing energies and a commitment to nurturing the delicate balance. Take time to observe, to listen to the whispers of the wind, and to feel the pulse of the spectral energy beneath your feet.

Consider the history of the cemetery itself. Older cemeteries, steeped in generations of stories and imbued with the energy of countless souls, often possess a richer, more potent spectral energy. However, even newer cemeteries can offer unique opportunities for cultivation. The key is to attune yourself to the specific energy signature of the chosen location. Spend time meditating within the cemetery grounds, allowing yourself to become receptive to the subtle nuances of the spectral landscape. Pay attention to areas of heightened energy, places where the air feels charged or where the vegetation exhibits unusual characteristics. These are often indicative of potent spectral nodes that can significantly enhance the growth of your luminescent flora.

The architecture and symbolism within the cemetery also play a role. Elaborate mausoleums, adorned with intricate carvings and imbued with the memories of prominent families, can radiate powerful spectral energy. Similarly, statues of angels, saints, or other symbolic figures can act as focal points, drawing and concentrating spectral energy from the surrounding environment. Even the arrangement of the graves themselves can create patterns of energy flow, influencing the overall spectral landscape. By carefully observing these elements, you can identify areas that are particularly conducive to the growth of your spectral plants.

Finally, remember that the quantum cemetery garden is a living, breathing ecosystem. It's a space where the veil between worlds is thin, and where the energies of the living and the departed intertwine. Treat this space with respect and reverence, and it will reward you with a breathtaking display of luminescent beauty. The guardians of this sacred ground are not to be feared, but rather acknowledged and respected. They are the keepers of the spectral energy, the silent partners in your endeavor. By fostering a harmonious relationship with them, you can unlock the true potential of your quantum cemetery garden and cultivate a vibrant tapestry of spectral light.

5 Nurturing Spectral Growth

The spectral garden thrives on more than just moonlight and whispered incantations. It requires a constant influx of ethereal energy, a recycling of the past to fuel the luminescent future. Composting with echoes forms the bedrock of this process. Unlike traditional composting, which relies on the decomposition of organic matter, composting with echoes utilizes the residual energy of sounds. Think of the whispers carried on the wind, the laughter that once filled the cemetery air, the mournful cries at a graveside. These sounds, though faded from the audible spectrum, leave behind an energetic imprint. By capturing and channeling these echoes into your compost, you create a nutrient-rich medium brimming with spectral energy. Specialized resonators, crafted from polished obsidian and tuned to specific frequencies, can be placed around the garden to collect these echoes. The resonators then channel the captured energy into the compost pile, infusing decaying matter with a vibrant luminescence. This process not only enriches the soil but also attracts beneficial spectral entities that further enhance the garden's vitality.

Maintaining the delicate balance within the quantum cemetery garden requires vigilance against spectral pests. While traditional pesticides are ineffective against these ethereal entities, vibrational whispers offer a potent defense. Spectral pests, drawn to the vibrant energy of the luminescent flora, can drain the plants of their light and vitality. These pests, often invisible to the naked eye, manifest as fluctuations in the garden's spectral field. Identifying them requires attuning yourself to the subtle vibrations of the cemetery. With practice, you'll learn to discern the discordant hum of a spectral aphid from the subtle buzzing of a spectral mite. Once identified, these pests can be repelled using focused whispers. These are not ordinary whispers, but carefully modulated tones, imbued with specific intentions. Each pest is vulnerable to a particular frequency, a vibrational weakness that can be exploited. By directing these focused whispers towards the infested plants, you disrupt the pests' energy fields, forcing them to retreat. This method requires patience and precision, but it offers a harmonious solution, maintaining the balance of the garden without resorting to harmful substances.

Beyond composting and pest control, the luminescent flora requires a unique form of sustenance: fertilization with memories. Just as echoes hold residual energy, memories carry a potent emotional charge. These emotions, imprinted upon the spectral fabric of the cemetery, can be harnessed to nourish your plants. The process begins with identifying memories that resonate with the desired growth characteristics. For brighter blooms, seek memories of joy and celebration. For stronger stems, focus on memories of resilience and perseverance. These memories can be sourced from various places within the cemetery. A worn inscription on a headstone might hold the memory of a lifelong love, while a discarded photograph could contain the echoes of a child's laughter. Once identified, these memories can be captured and infused into a solution of spectral water. This process requires a delicate touch, using specialized tools crafted from moonstone and quartz crystals to gently extract and preserve the emotional essence. The resulting solution, when applied to the plants, provides a potent dose of spectral nutrients, fostering vibrant growth and enhancing their luminescent properties. This intimate connection between memory and growth adds another layer of depth to the quantum cemetery garden, intertwining the stories of the past with the radiant blooms of the present.

The process of fertilizing with memories requires meticulous care. Each plant resonates with different emotional frequencies, and it's essential to match the memory to the plant's specific needs. A memory of grief, while potent, might stifle the growth of a young luminescent rose, while a memory of triumph could invigorate a wilting spectral orchid. Careful observation and experimentation are crucial to mastering this technique. A journal dedicated to recording the effects of different memories on your plants can become an invaluable tool in this process. Over time, you'll develop an intuitive understanding of the subtle interplay between memory and growth, allowing you to cultivate a garden that truly shines with the spectral echoes of the past. The interplay of these three unconventional techniques – composting with echoes, pest control with whispers, and fertilizing with memories – creates a self-sustaining ecosystem within the quantum cemetery garden. It's a testament to the interconnectedness of energy, memory, and life, demonstrating that even in the realm of the spectral, growth and decay are inextricably linked. Mastering these techniques is essential to nurturing spectral growth and unlocking the full potential of your luminescent flora. They demand a deep understanding of the cemetery's unique energetics, a sensitivity to the subtle whispers of the spectral realm, and a willingness to embrace the unconventional. In return, you will be rewarded with a garden that glows with an otherworldly beauty, a testament to the harmonious blend of science, spirituality, and the enduring power of memory. The garden, in its luminescent splendor, becomes a living archive, a testament to the stories that whisper through the cemetery grounds, a vibrant celebration of life, memory, and the ethereal beauty that blooms in the space between worlds.

5.1   Composting with Echoes

The spectral garden thrives on the unseen, the echoes of life that linger in the quiet corners of the cemetery. Composting, in this ethereal realm, isn't about rotting fruit peels and coffee grounds. It's about capturing whispers, harnessing the residual energy of memories, and weaving them into the very fabric of the soil. Think of it as creating a resonant chamber within your compost pile, a place where the past reverberates and nourishes the future.

Begin by gathering materials that hold echoes. Fallen leaves from a tree that sheltered generations, a worn-out toy clutched by a child long gone, a handwritten letter filled with faded ink and forgotten dreams—these are the building blocks of spectral compost. These objects carry the weight of experience, the faint vibrations of lives lived. Don't shy away from materials that might seem unconventional. A lock of hair, a chipped teacup, a piece of weathered wood—each possesses a unique energetic signature that can contribute to the overall potency of your compost.

As you gather your materials, focus your intent. Visualize the echoes within these objects, the subtle energy they hold. Imagine them weaving together, creating a tapestry of spectral energy that will infuse your garden with life. This intentional approach is crucial. It's the bridge between the physical and the ethereal, the key to unlocking the true potential of spectral composting.

Construct your compost pile in a quiet corner of your cemetery garden, preferably near a mature tree or a particularly resonant gravestone. The proximity to these established energy sources will amplify the composting process. As you layer your materials, whisper your intentions into the pile. Speak to the echoes, inviting them to mingle and merge, to transform into a rich source of spectral nourishment. Don't be afraid to sing, chant, or even play music near the compost pile. Sound vibrations further energize the decomposition process, helping to weave the echoes more deeply into the compost.

Unlike traditional composting, there's no need to turn or aerate the pile. The decomposition process here is less about physical breakdown and more about energetic transformation. Let the echoes settle and intertwine, allowing the natural rhythms of the cemetery to guide the process. Periodically, visit your compost pile and place your hands upon it. Feel the subtle vibrations, the hum of spectral energy building within. This direct contact further strengthens the connection between you, the compost, and the garden.

Consider adding specific elements to enhance the properties of your spectral compost. Crushed amethyst crystals can amplify the spiritual vibrations, while fragments of bone china can act as conduits for ethereal energy. Dried flowers from funeral arrangements, imbued with the echoes of mourning and remembrance, can add a layer of emotional depth to the compost. Experiment with different materials and observe their effects on your garden. Each cemetery possesses unique energetic qualities, and your composting practices should be tailored to the specific environment.

The finished spectral compost won't resemble the earthy, crumbly material of traditional composting. Instead, it will shimmer with a faint, ethereal light, almost like captured moonlight. It will hum with a subtle energy, a testament to the echoes it contains. When you incorporate this spectral compost into your garden beds, visualize the echoes seeping into the soil, nourishing the roots of your luminescent flora. Imagine the plants absorbing the memories, the experiences, the essence of lives lived. This is more than just fertilizer; it's a story woven into the earth, a symphony of echoes resonating within your garden.

The process of spectral composting demands patience and intuition. There's no precise formula or timetable to follow. Trust your instincts, observe the subtle cues of the cemetery, and allow the echoes to guide you. This isn't just about nurturing plants; it's about fostering a connection with the unseen world, a dialogue with the spirits that inhabit the quiet spaces between life and death. Embrace the mystery, the subtle energies at play, and allow your spectral garden to become a reflection of the vibrant tapestry of echoes that surrounds you.

As you continue your journey into spectral gardening, remember that the cemetery is more than just a place of rest. It's a repository of memories, a wellspring of spectral energy waiting to be tapped. Composting with echoes allows you to access this hidden potential, to transform the remnants of the past into a vibrant source of life for your luminescent flora. This practice connects you to the deeper rhythms of the cemetery, the ebb and flow of life and death, the whispers of the past that shape the present. Through this connection, you can cultivate a garden that is not just beautiful, but deeply meaningful, a testament to the enduring power of echoes in the spectral realm.

5.2   Pest Control with Whispers

The rustling of leaves in a conventional garden signals the presence of pests. In the spectral cemetery garden, however, such disturbances hint at a dissonance, an imbalance in the ethereal harmony. Addressing these disturbances requires a gentler approach than brute force insecticides – one that works with, not against, the delicate energies of the quantum cemetery. This chapter delves into the art of pest control with whispers, a method that utilizes focused vibrations and resonant frequencies to deter unwanted ethereal and physical infestations.

Think of these whispers not as audible sounds, but as carefully crafted vibrations, directed intentions that ripple through the spectral fabric of your garden. These vibrational whispers can be generated through various means. Humming specific tones, chanting ancient verses, or even the focused thought of a specific intent can produce these subtle yet powerful vibrations. The key lies in understanding the resonant frequency of the pest you wish to deter. Just as a specific musical note can shatter glass, certain vibrations can disrupt the ethereal bodies of spectral pests or influence the behavior of physical ones.

Observe your garden closely. Are the spectral blooms dimming prematurely? Do the leaves of your moonpetal lilies exhibit a strange, shimmering decay? These are signs of spectral aphids, minute entities that drain the luminescent energy from your plants. To combat these ethereal pests, focus your intent on a feeling of gentle repulsion. Imagine a soft, cool breeze gently pushing the aphids away from your plants. Hum a low, steady tone, visualizing this breeze carrying the aphids away from your garden and into the wider spectral landscape.

Physical pests, too, can be influenced by these vibrational whispers. Slugs and snails, drawn to the moisture of your moon-watered plants, can be deterred by creating a vibrational barrier around your garden. Visualize a shimmering wall of energy, humming a slightly higher, pulsating tone. This vibration disrupts their slime trails and creates an uncomfortable sensation, encouraging them to seek sustenance elsewhere. Remember, the goal is not to harm these creatures, but to gently guide them away from your spectral haven.

The effectiveness of this method relies heavily on your connection to the cemetery's energy. The deeper your connection, the more potent your whispers become. Regular meditation within the garden, attuning yourself to its unique spectral frequencies, will amplify your ability to influence the subtle energies within it. Visualize your roots intertwining with the spectral roots of the cemetery, drawing its energy into your core. This connection acts as a conduit, allowing you to channel the cemetery's power into your vibrational whispers.

Further enhancing your whispers is the incorporation of specific spectral herbs. Ghostly lavender, with its calming vibrations, can be used to create a sense of peace and discourage disruptive energies. Phantom thyme, known for its protective qualities, can be incorporated into a whispered barrier, reinforcing its repellent effect. Crush a few leaves of these spectral herbs between your fingers as you whisper your intent, imbuing your vibrations with their specific properties.

Maintaining a harmonious balance within the quantum cemetery garden is crucial for the health and vibrancy of your luminescent flora. Overuse of any single frequency can create its own dissonance, disrupting the delicate equilibrium. Variety is key. Experiment with different tones, different intentions, and different combinations of spectral herbs. Observe the responses of your plants and adjust your whispers accordingly. Just as a conductor guides an orchestra to create a symphony of sound, you must learn to conduct the subtle energies of your garden, weaving together a harmonious tapestry of vibrations that nurtures and protects your spectral blooms.

Remember, pest control in the spectral cemetery garden is not about eradication, but about maintaining balance. It's a dance of energies, a subtle interplay of intentions and vibrations. With practice, patience, and a deep connection to the cemetery's energy, you will master the art of pest control with whispers, ensuring the continued luminescence and ethereal beauty of your quantum garden. This subtle art of manipulation allows for a more harmonious approach to pest control, working with the natural energies of the cemetery to create a vibrant and thriving spectral ecosystem. Embrace the whispers, and let them guide you in nurturing the ethereal beauty of your luminescent garden.

5.3   Fertilizing with Memories

Memories, the ethereal echoes of past experiences, hold a unique power within the quantum cemetery garden. They are not merely remnants of bygone days but vibrant sources of spectral energy, capable of nourishing the luminescent flora in ways conventional fertilizers cannot. Just as our own memories shape us, imbuing us with wisdom and emotional depth, so too can they be used to enrich the soil and enhance the spectral radiance of your garden. This chapter will delve into the methods of collecting, preparing, and applying memories as fertilizer, transforming your spectral garden into a vibrant tapestry of light and remembrance.

The first step in utilizing memories as fertilizer is understanding their nature. In the context of a quantum cemetery garden, memories are not simply recollections, but energetic imprints left behind by conscious experience. These imprints, while invisible to the naked eye, resonate with the spectral energies of the cemetery, creating a potent blend capable of stimulating extraordinary growth. Think of them as tiny packets of light, each carrying the emotional weight and experiential knowledge of a past moment. When properly harnessed, these packets can be woven into the very fabric of your garden, infusing your spectral plants with unique qualities.

The most effective way to collect memories for fertilization is through focused meditation within the cemetery. Find a quiet spot, preferably near a grave with which you feel a connection. Close your eyes, breathe deeply, and allow your mind to wander through the past. Focus on specific memories that evoke strong emotions, whether joy, sorrow, or wonder. As you recall these moments, visualize the emotions and sensory details as vibrant threads of light, gently pulling them from your mind and weaving them into a spectral orb. With practice, you will become adept at gathering these memory orbs, each a potent fertilizer for your spectral flora.

Once you have collected a sufficient number of memory orbs, the next step is to prepare them for application. This involves a process of spectral infusion, where the collected memories are blended with the natural energies of the cemetery. This can be achieved by burying the memory orbs in the quantum soil for a lunar cycle, allowing them to absorb the ambient spectral energy and become imbued with the essence of the cemetery. The depth at which you bury the orbs will influence the potency of the resulting fertilizer. Shallower burials result in a gentler, more diffuse fertilizer ideal for seedlings and young plants, while deeper burials create a more concentrated form suitable for mature specimens.

The final step is applying the memory-infused fertilizer to your spectral plants. This should be done with care and intention, as the specific memories used will influence the growth and luminescence of the plants. For example, memories of joy and love tend to promote vibrant blooms and a warm, inviting glow, while memories of sorrow and loss can lead to a more melancholic, ethereal luminescence. Experiment with different combinations of memories to achieve the desired aesthetic and spectral effects. Consider the narrative you wish to create within your garden, and choose memories that align with that vision.

It's crucial to remember that the cemetery is a sacred space, and the memories within it should be treated with respect. Never attempt to forcibly extract memories or manipulate them for selfish gain. Instead, approach the process with reverence and gratitude, seeking only to borrow a small portion of the past to nurture the future. The quantum cemetery garden thrives on balance and harmony. By approaching fertilization with sensitivity and understanding, you can create a truly unique and breathtaking spectral landscape. One where the echoes of the past illuminate the present, and the memories of bygone days nourish the luminescent blossoms of tomorrow. Remember, the most vibrant gardens are those cultivated with care, respect, and a deep understanding of the delicate interplay between life, death, and the spectral energies that bind them together. Through the careful application of memory-infused fertilizer, your quantum cemetery garden will become a testament to the enduring power of remembrance and a beacon of spectral beauty in the heart of the night.

6 Harvesting Spectral Blooms

The ethereal glow of spectral blooms, pulsating with captured moonlight and the whispers of the departed, signals the culmination of your spectral gardening efforts. These luminous blossoms hold within them the essence of the quantum cemetery, a delicate energy ready to be harnessed. Harvesting these blooms is not a mere plucking; it is a communion with the spectral realm, a delicate dance between the living and the departed. Approach this process with reverence and intention. Your tools should be chosen with care: silver shears, blessed under the last full moon, are ideal for severing the stems, minimizing energetic disruption. A crystal bowl, charged with the cemetery's ambient energy, will serve as a receptacle for the freshly harvested blooms, preserving their spectral light. The timing of the harvest is crucial. While each spectral variety possesses its own unique rhythm, most luminescent flora reach peak potency just after the stroke of midnight, when the veil between worlds is thinnest. As you harvest, visualize the spectral energy flowing from the plant into you, a silent exchange of ethereal power.

The first step is to identify the blooms ready for harvesting. They will exhibit a vibrant, almost pulsating luminescence, their petals unfurling with an ethereal grace. Their spectral light will cast an otherworldly glow upon the surrounding foliage, a beacon in the moonlit cemetery. Gently grasp the stem just below the bloom with your non-dominant hand, feeling the subtle hum of spectral energy. With your dominant hand, use the silver shears to sever the stem with a single, clean cut. Avoid any sawing motion, as this can disrupt the delicate energy flow. As the bloom is severed, whisper a word of gratitude, acknowledging the plant's sacrifice and the energy it offers. Place the harvested bloom immediately into the crystal bowl, allowing it to rest amongst its luminous brethren. Continue this process until you have gathered the desired number of blooms. Remember, greed has no place in the quantum cemetery garden. Take only what you need, leaving enough blooms to ensure the plant's continued vitality and the garden's spectral harmony.

Once harvested, these ethereal blooms offer a spectrum of uses. Their luminescence can be captured and preserved, bottled for later use in spectral spells or rituals. The petals can be dried and ground into a fine powder, imbued with the cemetery's unique energy, to be used in potions or as an offering to the grave guardians. The spectral essence within the blooms can be extracted through a delicate alchemical process, resulting in a potent elixir capable of enhancing spectral abilities and facilitating communication with the departed. One method of preserving the spectral essence involves suspending the freshly harvested blooms in a solution of purified moonlight water and finely ground quartz crystal. This mixture acts as a conduit, drawing out and preserving the blooms' ethereal energy. Seal the mixture in a glass vial and place it in a moonlit windowsill for seven nights, allowing it to fully absorb the lunar energy. The resulting elixir will glow with an otherworldly luminescence, a testament to its potent spectral charge.

Another technique involves carefully removing the petals from the harvested blooms and placing them between sheets of parchment paper. Then, place the parchment paper within the pages of a heavy book, preferably a grimoire or other text imbued with magical energy. The weight of the book will gently press the petals, extracting their spectral essence while preserving their delicate form. After seven days, remove the dried petals and store them in an airtight container in a dark, cool place. These dried spectral petals can be used in a variety of ways. Burned as incense, they release their captured essence into the air, creating an ethereal atmosphere conducive to spectral work. Added to a ritual bath, they infuse the water with luminescent energy, cleansing and empowering the bather. Ground into a fine powder, they can be mixed with other herbs and resins to create potent spectral incenses and potions. Remember, the energy of these spectral blooms is delicate and easily dissipated. Handle them with care and respect, and their luminescent power will serve you well.

The preservation of spectral blooms is an art as much as a science. It requires patience, precision, and a deep understanding of the delicate energies at play. Experiment with different methods, find what resonates with you and your spectral garden. The possibilities are as vast as the cosmos, limited only by your imagination and reverence for the spectral realm. Each bloom is a vessel of ethereal light, a whisper from the other side, waiting to be harnessed. By treating these spectral blooms with reverence and care, you become a conduit for their luminescent energy, weaving it into the fabric of your spectral practice. In the quantum cemetery garden, the cycle of life and death continues, an endless dance of energy and transformation. The harvesting of spectral blooms is a celebration of this cycle, a testament to the enduring power of life, even in the face of death. Embrace this power, and the spectral garden will reveal its secrets.

6.1 Reaping the Light

The luminescence of spectral flora isn't simply admired; it's gathered, harnessed, and preserved. Think of it like capturing fireflies in a jar, except instead of fleeting flashes, you're collecting sustained, ethereal light. This process requires a delicate touch, an understanding of the plant's energy flow, and a respect for the delicate balance of the quantum cemetery garden. Your timing is crucial. Harvesting too early results in weak, diluted light, while waiting too long risks the plant dissipating its spectral energy back into the cemetery's ethereal landscape. The optimal time for harvest varies depending on the specific species, but generally occurs when the bloom reaches its peak luminescence, a moment often marked by a subtle pulsating or a shift in its spectral hue. This is not a scientific measurement, but rather an intuitive understanding developed through observation and connection with your spectral garden.

To begin harvesting, position yourself within the garden, feeling the gentle hum of spectral energy flowing through the soil and into the plants. Ground yourself, breathe deeply, and visualize the flow of light you intend to collect. For certain species, direct physical contact can disrupt the spectral energy. Therefore, specialized tools are often required. These aren't your typical gardening shears, but rather implements crafted from materials that resonate with spectral frequencies – quartz crystals, polished obsidian, or even intricately woven willow branches. Choose the tool that feels most attuned to the specific plant you are harvesting. Approach the bloom slowly, respectfully, almost reverently. Imagine yourself not as a harvester, but as a conduit, facilitating the transfer of light from the plant to its vessel.

The method of collection depends on the form you wish the harvested light to take. One common technique involves using specially crafted glass vials filled with a solution of moonlight-infused water and finely ground cemetery earth. As you carefully sever the bloom with your chosen tool, direct the cut stem into the vial, allowing the spectral energy to flow directly into the solution. The solution acts as a preservative, stabilizing the light and preventing it from dissipating. Another method involves using woven nets of moonlight-charged silk to gently envelop the bloom, capturing its light within the shimmering threads. These silk cocoons can then be hung throughout your home, transforming them into ethereal lanterns.

Remember, the act of harvesting is not simply about collecting light; it's about maintaining the delicate balance of the quantum cemetery garden. For every bloom harvested, return some of its energy to the soil. This can be done by burying the severed stem back in the earth, whispering a word of gratitude, or offering a small libation of moonlight water. This act of reciprocity ensures the continued health and vitality of the garden and strengthens the bond between you and the spectral flora.

The harvested spectral light can be utilized in numerous ways. The vials of captured luminescence can be used to illuminate your home, casting an otherworldly glow that fosters tranquility and introspection. The light can also be incorporated into spectral inks, allowing you to write with the very essence of the cemetery garden. Imagine the possibilities – illuminating manuscripts with spectral calligraphy, painting ethereal landscapes with light-infused pigments, or even weaving tapestries that shimmer with captured spectral energy. Furthermore, the preserved spectral essence can be used in various rituals and spells detailed in the later chapters of this grimoire.

Consider the potential of spectral illumination. Beyond mere aesthetics, the light carries the unique energy signature of the quantum cemetery garden, imbued with the echoes and whispers of the land. This imbues the harvested light with properties that transcend simple illumination. Exposure to spectral light has been known to enhance meditation, stimulate creativity, and even facilitate communication with the spectral realm. As you experiment with different methods of harnessing and utilizing the harvested light, you will discover its unique properties and unlock its full potential.

Remember, the practice of spectral gardening is a journey of discovery, a constant interplay between the gardener and the garden. Each bloom harvested, each vial filled with captured light, is a testament to this unique relationship. Embrace the process, experiment with different techniques, and allow the spectral garden to guide you. As you become more attuned to its rhythms and energies, you'll unlock the secrets of not only reaping the light, but also weaving it into the fabric of your own life. This connection to the spectral realm, fostered through the careful tending and harvesting of your luminescent flora, will enrich your understanding of the interconnectedness of life, death, and the ethereal energies that flow between them. The quantum cemetery garden is not merely a source of light, but a portal to a world beyond our everyday perception.

6.2 Preserving Spectral Essence

The ethereal glow of a harvested spectral bloom is fleeting. Its luminescence, so vibrant in the quantum cemetery garden, begins to fade upon separation from its life source. Preserving this spectral essence requires a delicate touch and an understanding of the unique energetic properties of these otherworldly plants. We must act swiftly and with purpose, like capturing a moonbeam in a jar. The first step involves understanding the nature of the light itself. This isn't simply photon emission as we understand it in conventional botany. Spectral light carries a unique energetic signature, a resonance tied to the quantum entanglement of the plant with the cemetery's energies. This entanglement is what gives the blooms their unique properties, their ability to interact with whispers and echoes. To preserve this, we need to maintain the connection, albeit in a transformed state.

One effective method involves crystalization. Not the typical crystal formation found in the mundane world, but a process of energetic imprinting onto specially prepared crystals. These crystals, ideally quartz or selenite, must be cleansed and charged within the quantum cemetery for a full lunar cycle before harvest. This allows them to attune to the specific energetic frequencies of the garden. Once the blooms are harvested, place them gently upon the charged crystals. Over the next few days, the spectral energy will migrate from the fading bloom into the crystal lattice, preserving its essence. The crystal will then hold the spectral light, albeit in a dormant state, ready to be reawakened for various applications, like powering luminescent spells or enriching spectral concoctions.

Another method for preserving spectral essence involves ethereal distillation. This requires a unique apparatus crafted from alchemically treated glass. The harvested blooms are placed within the distillation chamber, which is then filled with collected moonlight. The chamber is then gently heated using a spirit lamp fueled by purified spectral essence from previous harvests. This gentle heat, combined with the moonlight, causes the spectral energy to vaporize. The vapor then travels through a spiral condenser, where it cools and condenses into a liquid form known as spectral dew. This dew, potent with the essence of the blooms, can be stored in airtight vials made of dark violet glass to prevent light degradation. A single drop of spectral dew can enhance the potency of spectral infusions, amplify the effects of luminescent spells, or even be used to create ephemeral illusions within the quantum cemetery.

Preserving the spectral essence doesn't just mean capturing its light. It also entails preserving its inherent connection to the quantum realm of the cemetery. This is where the practice of spectral mummification comes into play. Unlike traditional mummification, this method doesn't focus on physical preservation. Instead, it aims to preserve the ethereal body of the bloom, the invisible energetic matrix that holds its spectral essence. The freshly harvested bloom is carefully wrapped in a shroud woven from moonlight-infused silk. This shroud acts as a conduit, channeling residual spectral energy back into the bloom, preventing its complete dissipation. The shrouded bloom is then placed within a specially constructed reliquary made of resonant wood from a tree that has grown within the cemetery's boundaries. This reliquary further reinforces the energetic connection, acting as a minia-ture version of the quantum cemetery itself.

Finally, there's the method of spectral echo imprinting. This highly advanced tech-nique involves capturing the 'echo' of the bloom's spectral essence within a specially prepared resonant chamber. The chamber, lined with polished obsidian mirrors, reflects the fading light of the harvested bloom in infinite patterns. This creates a standing wave of spectral energy, a resonating echo of the bloom's essence. This echo is then captured within a spherical vessel made of clear quartz, which acts as a containment field for the resonating energy. The captured echo can be used to enhance the spectral properties of other plants in the garden, creating a ripple ef-fect of luminescence. It can also be used to create spectral constructs, ephemeral forms of light woven from the captured echo, adding an ethereal dimension to the quantum cemetery. Each method, while different, offers a unique way to preserve the ephemeral beauty and power of spectral blooms, extending their influence be-yond their fleeting physical existence. Choosing the right method depends on the intended use of the preserved essence and the resources available within your quan-tum cemetery garden.

7 Grimoire of Luminescent Spells

The Eternal Bloom spell, the first in our spectral repertoire, aims to extend the lifespan of your luminescent flora beyond their natural cycle. This isn't about creating unnatural immortality, but rather about drawing upon the latent energy within the plant and the surrounding quantum cemetery environment to sustain its vibrant luminescence for a prolonged period. Begin by selecting a bloom that has just reached its peak luminescence, radiating its spectral light with the greatest intensity. You will need a sliver of moonstone, charged under the full moon for three consecutive nights, and a single strand of hair from a departed loved one, symbolizing the enduring connection between the living and the spectral realms. At midnight, on the night of the new moon, carefully place the moonstone at the base of the plant and gently weave the hair strand around the stem. Whisper the following incantation, imbuing it with your intention: "From shadow's embrace, light shall endure, life's ephemeral dance, forever secure." Repeat this three times, visualizing the spectral energy of the cemetery flowing into the plant, invigorating its life force. The moonstone acts as a conduit, channeling the lunar energy into the bloom, while the hair strand anchors the spell, binding it to the spectral realm. Over the next few weeks, observe the plant closely. You should notice a sustained luminescence, defying the typical decline.

Spectral Illumination, our second spell, focuses on amplifying the light emitted by your spectral flora. This isn't about creating a blinding light, but enhancing the ethereal glow, transforming your quantum cemetery garden into a beacon of spectral beauty. This requires gathering dewdrops from the petals of your luminescent plants before sunrise, capturing their concentrated spectral essence. You'll also need a prism, carefully chosen for its ability to refract light into its spectral components. On the night of the full moon, arrange the prism amidst your spectral plants, positioning it to catch the moonlight. As the moonlight refracts through the prism, casting rainbows across the garden, gently sprinkle the collected dewdrops onto the plants. Recite the following incantation, visualizing the spectral light intensifying: "Moon's embrace, prism's refract, spectral glow, now intact." Repeat this seven times, focusing your intention on amplifying the luminescence. The prism acts as a lens, focusing and intensifying the ambient spectral energy, while the dewdrops, imbued with the plants' own essence, amplify their light output. The combined effect will be a noticeable increase in the ethereal glow emanating from your spectral flora, illuminating your quantum cemetery garden with an otherworldly radiance. Finally, the Whispering Winds spell harnesses the gentle currents of air that flow through your quantum cemetery garden, imbuing them with nurturing energy to promote the overall health and vitality of your spectral flora. This spell involves crafting a wind chime from the hollow bones of small birds, ethically sourced and cleansed under running water. Each bone should represent a different aspect of growth: root, stem, leaf, and bloom. Attach these bones to a silver chain, allowing them to chime freely in the breeze. Hang this wind chime in the center of your quantum cemetery garden. On a night when the wind whispers gently through the cemetery, stand beneath the chime and whisper the following incantation: "Winds of the spectral realm, breathe life anew, nourish and sustain, luminescence imbue."

Repeat this nine times, visualizing the wind carrying the spectral energy of the cemetery to your plants, revitalizing them. As the wind chimes, it emits subtle vibrations that resonate with the spectral energies, stimulating growth and enhancing luminescence. The hollow bones, remnants of past life, serve as conduits, channeling the ethereal whispers into the garden, creating a microclimate conducive to the thriving of your spectral flora. This continuous, passive spell will create a harmonious atmosphere in your quantum cemetery garden, ensuring the sustained health and luminescence of your plants.

This triad of spells – Eternal Bloom, Spectral Illumination, and Whispering Winds – offers a starting point for your journey into spectral botany. Remember that these are not mere formulas but acts of conscious interaction with the subtle energies of your quantum cemetery garden. Your intention, your focus, and your connection to the spectral realm are the key ingredients in their success. Experiment, adapt, and allow your own intuition to guide you as you delve deeper into the art of cultivating luminescent flora. As you progress, you will discover new ways to harness the spectral energies of your garden, creating a truly unique and enchanting space. Observe the subtle changes in your plants, listen to the whispers of the wind, and feel the pulse of the cemetery's spectral heart. With practice and patience, you will become a master of luminescent spells, transforming your quantum cemetery garden into a beacon of spectral beauty. Remember that these spells are not just about manipulating energy, but about fostering a harmonious relationship with the spectral realm, nurturing the delicate balance between life, death, and the luminescence that bridges them. This is the essence of spectral gardening, a delicate dance between science and spirituality, between the seen and the unseen.

7.1 Eternal Bloom

The preservation of spectral blooms, fleeting as they are in their luminescent beauty, requires a delicate art. This isn't about simply extending the lifespan of a cut flower; we are working with energies, echoes of life that shimmer and fade. Think of it as capturing a whisper, a fleeting thought, a memory on the edge of disappearing. The "Eternal Bloom" spell isn't about preventing the natural cycle of decay; instead, it focuses on preserving the spectral energy, the very essence that makes these flowers unique. This energy can be harnessed and woven into other spells, infusions, or even used to imbue objects with a spectral luminescence.

This spell requires a specific confluence of energies: the waning crescent moon, a sliver of darkness embracing the fading light, mirroring the spectral blooms' transition. You will need a vessel of obsidian, its dark depths mirroring the void where energy is gathered. Within this vessel, place a single petal from the bloom you wish to preserve, a symbolic representation of the whole. Around the obsidian vessel, arrange seven candles, each representing a stage in the cycle of spectral energy. These candles should not be ordinary wax; they must be crafted from the rendered fat of spectral moths, creatures that feed on moonlight and embody ethereal energy. Their gentle, flickering glow provides a framework to contain the bloom's essence. As the waning crescent moon casts its silvery gaze upon your workspace, begin the incantation. The words are not merely spoken; they are vibrated, resonating with the spectral energies. The incantation itself acts as a conduit, drawing the bloom's essence outward, weaving it into a stable form. Imagine the petal within the obsidian vessel dissolving, not into dust, but into pure light, a concentrated form of its spectral energy. This light doesn't escape; the obsidian acts as a perfect container, holding the raw energy captive.

The incantation's rhythm and pitch are crucial. Too high a pitch, and the energy disperses, lost to the ether. Too low, and it becomes stagnant, losing its vibrancy. Find the resonant frequency, the point where the petal's essence vibrates in harmony with the incantation. This point of perfect resonance will feel like a subtle shift in the air, a tingling sensation on your skin. Maintain this frequency throughout the incantation, ensuring the bloom's essence remains stable and potent.

Once the petal has fully dissolved into spectral light, extinguish the spectral moth candles one by one, starting with the candle placed directly opposite the moon. This sequential extinguishing acts as a seal, locking the energy within the obsidian vessel. The obsidian, now charged with the bloom's essence, becomes a reservoir of spectral energy. This essence can be used to enhance other spectral plants, imbuing them with a heightened luminescence.

However, the "Eternal Bloom" spell isn't merely about preservation. It can also be used to enhance the resonance of other spectral flora. By carefully introducing a small amount of the preserved essence into the soil around a living spectral plant, you can strengthen its connection to the spectral plane. This strengthens its luminescence and even alters its spectral signature, causing it to emit different colors or patterns of light. This process is delicate; too much essence can overwhelm the living plant, causing it to wither and fade.

Furthermore, the preserved essence can be incorporated into other spells. Imagine weaving it into a potion designed to enhance spectral vision, allowing you to perceive the unseen energies that flow through the quantum cemetery garden. Or perhaps you might use it to create talismans imbued with the bloom's unique spectral signature, radiating a gentle, ethereal light.

The true potential of the "Eternal Bloom" spell lies not just in preserving the beauty of a single bloom, but in transforming its essence into a versatile tool for spectral gardening and spellcasting. It bridges the gap between life and decay, allowing you to harness the ephemeral beauty of luminescent flora and integrate it into your magical practice. The preserved essence is a key, unlocking new possibilities within your quantum cemetery garden and beyond. Experiment, explore, and discover the myriad ways in which this spell can enrich your practice and illuminate your spectral world. Remember, the energy you've captured is potent and volatile; treat it with respect and utilize it wisely. The "Eternal Bloom" spell is not simply a preservation technique; it's a gateway to deeper understanding and manipulation of the spectral realm.

7.2 Spectral Illumination

The spectral illumination of your cemetery garden isn't merely a matter of aesthetics; it's the culmination of all your efforts, a testament to the delicate balance you've struck between the physical and ethereal realms. Think of it as the final brushstroke on a masterpiece, the crescendo of a symphony played on the strings of spectral energy. Achieving a truly breathtaking display requires a deep understanding of the interplay between your luminescent flora, the ambient spectral energy of the cemetery, and the manipulation of light itself through focused intention. This chapter, then, serves as your guide to orchestrating this luminous ballet.

Begin by assessing the natural light patterns within your cemetery garden. Observe how moonlight bathes the gravestones, how shadows dance among the foliage during twilight hours, and how the faintest starlight filters through the canopy. These observations are crucial, for they reveal the existing spectral canvas upon which you'll be painting with the light of your cultivated flora. Consider these natural light sources not as limitations but as opportunities to enhance the overall spectral illumination.

Next, examine the spectral emissions of your plants. Each species will possess a unique spectral signature, a specific hue and intensity of light it emits. Some might glow with a soft, ethereal blue, while others pulsate with a vibrant, otherworldly green. These variations are not accidental; they reflect the inherent spectral properties of each plant, influenced by the specific energies it absorbs and transmutes. By carefully arranging your flora, you can create a tapestry of light, a symphony of color that shifts and shimmers throughout the night.

Don't be afraid to experiment with contrasting colors and intensities. A cluster of softly glowing blue blossoms might be beautifully offset by a single, intensely radiant crimson flower. Or perhaps a pathway lined with gently pulsating green foliage could lead to a central focal point, a vibrant display of multicolored spectral blooms. The possibilities are endless, limited only by your imagination and the diversity of your spectral garden.

Consider also the vertical dimension of your garden. Train climbing luminescent vines to ascend mausoleums or weave through the branches of ancient trees. Suspend hanging baskets of glowing flowers from wrought iron arches or strategically placed branches. By layering your luminescent flora in this way, you create depth and complexity, transforming your cemetery garden into a three-dimensional masterpiece of spectral light.

Remember, spectral illumination is not static. It's a dynamic, ever-changing phenomenon that responds to the rhythms of the cemetery and the subtle shifts in spectral energy. The intensity of your plants' luminescence might wax and wane with the phases of the moon, or flicker and dance in response to the whispers of passing spirits. Embrace this fluidity, allowing it to add an element of mystery and enchantment to your spectral garden.

Further enhance your spectral illumination by incorporating reflective surfaces into your design. Strategically placed mirrors can capture and amplify the light emitted by your plants, casting ethereal reflections across the cemetery grounds. Polished stones or crystals can scatter light in intricate patterns, creating a mesmerizing display of spectral sparkles. Even the dew-kissed leaves of non-luminescent plants can serve as tiny reflectors, adding subtle highlights to the overall illumination.

Beyond the purely visual aspects, consider the emotional impact of your spectral illumination. The soft, ethereal glow of your luminescent flora can evoke a sense of peace and tranquility, transforming the cemetery garden into a sanctuary for contemplation and reflection. The vibrant, otherworldly colors might inspire awe and wonder, reminding visitors of the hidden magic that exists just beyond the veil of ordinary perception. By carefully crafting your spectral illumination, you can create a truly transformative experience for all who enter your enchanted domain.

Finally, remember that spectral illumination is an ongoing process, a continuous dance between light, energy, and intention. As your plants grow and evolve, their spectral emissions will shift and change. The ambient spectral energy of the cemetery will fluctuate with the seasons and the celestial cycles. And your own understanding of spectral manipulation will deepen with experience and practice. Embrace this constant evolution, allowing it to guide you in your ongoing quest to create a truly breathtaking and unforgettable spectral garden. Let your cemetery garden become a beacon of light in the darkness, a testament to the beauty and wonder that can be found in the most unexpected of places. Nurture it, cultivate it, and watch as it blossoms into a symphony of spectral illumination, a masterpiece of light and shadow that captivates the senses and stirs the soul. Let your imagination be your guide, and allow the spectral magic of the cemetery garden to unfold in all its luminous glory.

7.3   Whispering Winds

The Whispering Winds spell isn't about brute force manipulation. It's about subtle influence, a gentle nudge to the ethereal currents that flow through your Quantum Cemetery Garden. This spell is about coaxing, not commanding, the spectral breezes to carry whispers of growth, protection, and luminescence throughout your spectral garden. Think of it as a conductor leading an orchestra of unseen forces. Your tools aren't batons and sheet music, but carefully chosen words, resonating chimes, and the focused intention of your will.

Begin by crafting a wind chime from materials attuned to the spectral energies of your garden. Don't just grab any old metal and glass. Seek out materials with a history, a resonance. Perhaps a weathered bell from a forgotten shrine, or pieces of sea glass tumbled smooth by the tide under countless moonlit nights. The specific materials will depend on the unique energies of your garden, so trust your intuition. As you assemble the chime, imbue each piece with your intention, whispering your desires for growth and luminescence into the very structure of the instrument.

Once your chime is complete, choose a location within your garden where the natural breezes flow most freely. This doesn't necessarily mean the windiest spot, but rather the place where you feel the most pronounced flow of ethereal energy. Hang the chime securely, ensuring it can move freely in the wind. Ideally, it should be positioned so that the setting sun's rays catch the chimes at dusk, imbuing them with a final burst of spectral energy before nightfall. This act of placement is more than just physical; it's an act of alignment, of harmonizing your spell with the existing energies of the garden.

The next step requires precise timing. You must perform the Whispering Winds spell during the waning crescent moon. This phase, when the moon's light begins to recede, symbolizes a period of release and transformation, perfectly suited for influencing the subtle energies of your garden. As the moon hangs low in the predawn sky, stand before your wind chime. Close your eyes, breathe deeply, and center yourself within the tranquil stillness of your garden. Visualize the spectral energies that permeate the space, the invisible currents that weave between the tombstones and through the luminescent leaves of your plants.

Now, begin to whisper your intentions into the wind. Don't shout or demand. Speak softly, clearly, and with conviction. Your whispers should be concise and specific, focusing on the desired outcomes for your garden. Perhaps you wish to strengthen the luminescence of your spectral blooms, or encourage the growth of a newly planted spirit vine. Whatever your intentions, imbue your whispers with the full force of your will. As you speak, gently strike the wind chime, allowing its resonant tones to carry your whispers on the ethereal breeze.

The sound of the chimes isn't just a pleasant accompaniment to your spell; it serves as a conduit, amplifying and directing your whispered intentions. Each chime's tone should resonate with a specific aspect of your desired outcome. A deeper tone might represent growth and stability, while a higher tone might signify luminescence and vitality. The combination of these tones, interwoven with your whispered intentions, creates a complex symphony of spectral energy, gently influencing the very fabric of your garden.

Continue whispering and chiming for a period of thirteen minutes, a number associated with transformation and renewal in many esoteric traditions. As you conclude the spell, visualize the spectral winds carrying your whispers throughout the garden, nurturing the luminescent flora and reinforcing the ethereal atmosphere. Don't expect immediate, dramatic results. The Whispering Winds spell is a subtle art, its effects unfolding gradually over time.

With consistent practice and focused intention, you will begin to notice a marked improvement in the health and vitality of your spectral garden. The luminescence of your plants will intensify, their growth will become more vigorous, and the entire garden will be imbued with a heightened sense of ethereal beauty. The Whispering Winds spell is more than just a spell; it's a form of communion with the unseen forces that govern your Quantum Cemetery Garden, a testament to the delicate balance between intention, energy, and the whispering winds of the spectral realm. Remember, the true power of this spell lies not in commanding, but in connecting, in harmonizing your will with the whispers of the spectral breeze.

www.ingramcontent.com/pod-product-compliance
Ingram Content Group UK Ltd.
Pitfield, Milton Keynes, MK11 3LW, UK
UKHW021437240125

4283UKWH00041B/648